WM. B. EERDMANS
PUBLISHING CO.
*Grand Rapids, Michigan*

MARSHALL PICKERING
CHRISTIAN since 1794 PUBLISHERS

The Bible is the story of God's dealings with his people. This story is like a picture God painted for all the world to see. God wanted to show everyone, everywhere, how much he loves ordinary people, and how he can make wonderful things happen through ordinary lives.

Israel was the kind of nation whose laws and traditions gave men the leadership in government and family life. However, Israel's history is full of stories of women. Some of these women rose to become leaders. Others shaped and changed the life of their nation as they stayed in the background. These stories stress the unique influence that women can have on history.

In Israel, the influence of women might have been limited by the customs and laws of their country, or by personal things like the amount of money they had, the type of education, their husband's position, or the number of children in the family. But in these stories we meet woman after woman who, in spite of outward hindrances, was limited only by the degree of her faith in God or by the degree of her determination to use the gifts he gave her.

We hope this book will make you eager to be used by God, and help you to believe more than ever before that you can be all God made you to be.

**ESTHER**
*A woman who was as courageous as she was beautiful*
Retold by Marlee Alex
Illustrated by Tiziana Gironi
© Copyright 1986 by Scandinavia
Publishing House, Nørregade 32, DK-1165 Copenhagen K.
English language edition first published 1987
through special arrangement with Scandinavia
jointly by W. B. Eerdmans Publishing Co.,
255 Jefferson Ave. S.E. Grand Rapids, Michigan 49503
and
Marshall Pickering, 3 Beggarwood Lane, Basingstoke,
Hants RG23 7LP, England
All rights reserved
Printed in Singapore
Eerdmans **ISBN 0-8028-5016-2**
Marshall **ISBN 0-551-014830**

# ESTHER

**A woman who was as courageous as she was beautiful**

*Retold by Marlee Alex*
*Illustrated by Tiziana Gironi*

**William B. Eerdmans Publishing Company**
**Grand Rapids, Michigan**

**Marshall Pickering**
**Basingstoke, England**

T he marble columns in the courtyard gleamed in the sunlight. It was high noon on the seventh day of the feast. The king's guests were half-drunk already. Some of them moved clumsily over the mosaic floors, floors that were magnificent even for the king of the vast Persian empire. Jewels and pearls sparkled among the other colored stones under their feet. Then King Ahasuerus swung his heavy golden wine goblet in the air and commanded his servants to fetch his wife, Queen Vashti.

The princes, noblemen and officers who were guests at the feast shouted. "Yes, bring the queen!" they exclaimed as they pulled away the purple linen drapes that shut off the inside of the palace. "She is more beautiful than all the other royal treasures put together!"

4

The servants hurried to the banquet room where the queen was entertaining the ladies. But they returned without her.

"What?" exclaimed King Ahasuerus. "The queen refuses to come?"

The king was embarrassed in front of his guests. And he was angry. He, the most powerful man in an empire that stretched from India to Ethiopia, was a man whom all others were eager to please. He was accustomed to having his every wish instantly fulfilled. Yet, now his own wife ignored him.

He gathered the princes and noblemen around him. "What should I do about this insulting behavior of the queen?" he asked.

"Well, you'll have to do something about it, Ahasuerus," the men complained. "If your wife disobeys you, then our wives are likely to start treating us in the same way. Soon, women all over the empire will begin to nag their husbands."

"Send her away!" insisted one of the princes. "And tell everyone why you are doing it."

So the king sent a decree throughout the empire, translated into each language of each province. It stated that every man must take charge of his household in an orderly manner and must not allow his wife to disobey. Of course, the king knew that he had to set the example. So Queen Vashti was banished from the empire.

Not too many days passed, however, before King Ahasuerus was sorry about what he had done. He missed his wife. In order to cheer him up, his noblemen suggested that a new queen be chosen. They proposed that a search be made far and wide, and that the prettiest maidens found in the empire be brought to the palace for one year. They were to be pampered like princesses, treated with the most expensive perfumes, facial creams,

and make-up, and then presented to the king one by one. When the king had seen all the young women, he could choose the one he liked best to be his queen.

King Ahasuerus was delighted with the idea. He felt certain that he could find a woman just as beautiful as his former queen, and one who would never make a fool of him. To ensure this, he would set up strict regulations about when she was allowed to see him, and about what was expected of her. And so, the king announced that a beauty contest was to be held at the palace.

7

There was a man named Mordecai living in the capital city, not far from the palace. He was a Jew, a descendant of the Israelites. In this man's home lived a young woman named Esther. She was a cousin of Mordecai whom he had taken into his household when she was small and raised as his own daughter.

Esther's skin was smooth as silk, her complexion, a tawny olive. Her eyes were large and expressive, framed by a thick rim of dark lashes. "She qualifies for the beauty contest," said the king's men. And she was the first one chosen.

Esther was a high-spirited young woman, but her zest was tempered by grace and kindness. She soon became a favorite of Hegai, the servant who was in charge of all the maidens. Esther was given the nicest room at the palace, and seven maids to wait upon her and to lavish her with beauty treatments. She was given the first choice of exotic fruits and of luxurious clothes.

In spite of this, her cousin Mordecai was worried about her. He had no choice but to let her go, but he gave her instructions not to reveal that she was Jewish. Every day he took a walk past the garden fence near her window. At those times he was comforted by her smile and the happy expression on her face.

9

At last the day arrived when Esther was to meet the king. Hegai asked if she would like to choose for herself the clothes she wished to wear. "And choose some things from among this jewelry," he offered, handing her an ornately hand-carved wooden box. The box was edged by rows of emeralds and rubies.

Esther carefully set the box down on her dresser and lifted its heavy lid. The contents of the box stunned her. It was full of necklaces, rings, brooches, bracelets, pearls to drape in the hair, and jeweled combs to set it with. Esther had never seen anything so magnificent. Her fingers caressed the sparkling jewels as she turned to Hegai.

"I am from an ordinary family," she replied. "Why should I pretend to be rich and important? If I am to wear any of this, then you must choose it for me."

Hegai drew out a single strand of glistening pearls and hung it around her neck. Then he chose for her a silk dress without trim. It fit her perfectly. Hegai knew that the simplest clothing would make the king notice Esther's natural beauty, the kind of beauty which shines from the inside out.

As Esther passed through long corridors on her way to the king's apartment, the palace servants stopped what they were doing to admire her. When the king set eyes on her, he knew he did not need to look further for his queen. He declared an official holiday throughout the empire, ordered a great feast at the palace and sent gifts to each province to celebrate his marriage to Esther.

The days and years of Esther's reign as queen passed quickly for her. During this time, her cousin Mordecai became an officer in the Imperial Guard just inside the palace gates. One day Mordecai overheard two of the other officers planning to kill the king. He told Esther about it, and she reported it. The king's life was saved, and Mordecai's name was recorded in the Imperial Record Book.

13

Not long afterward, the king appointed a new Chief of State whose name was Haman. Haman was proud. He wanted all servants and other officials to bow down whenever he passed by. Everyone was careful to do it, for Haman was a rough and cruel man. That is, everyone bowed down to Haman except Mordecai.

"I am a Jew," Mordecai insisted. "As a Jew, I cannot bow down to anyone except God."

This made Haman mad. He wanted to have Mordecai hanged to death. But he decided to do something even worse. He decided to have all the Jewish people in the empire killed. And he decided to make a game of it by throwing a pair of dice to determine the exact day it should happen. In this way he could spread terror and fear among them.

Haman told the king about his plan. "There is a race of people who do not

obey your laws," he argued. "These people should be destroyed. Otherwise all the people in the empire will begin to act the same way."

The king did not bother to ask for any details. "Do as you like," he said as he took off the ring that had his initials on it. He gave the ring to Haman to use to seal the death order, for the king was used to giving Haman whatever the man wanted.

Haman marched out happily. He sealed the order with the king's ring, and sent it by running messengers to the governors of each province. The order commanded them to kill all Jews, young and old, including women and children, on a certain day at a certain time. Haman promised the governors that they would be remembered as heroes for doing this.

15

The Jewish people in the capital city were the first to hear the order. They began to panic. When Mordecai heard about it, he ran through the streets, straight to the palace gates, shouting and crying. Hour by hour the news spread, until Jews everywhere became sick with terror. They refused to eat, they tore their clothes, and sprinkled themselves with ashes as a way of protesting to God and the king.

B ack at the palace, Queen Esther had not heard about the order to kill all Jews. No one, not even the king, had any idea that she was Jewish. She had been alone in her own apartment for more than thirty days. The king had not sent for her, and it was forbidden for her to even ask to see the king.

The days had been lonely for Esther. A sad feeling grew in her heart. It was as if the king had forgotten about her. She was afraid he was angry with her. The worry

and the hurt made her imagine that he was planning to send her away just as he had Queen Vashti.

Esther was supposed to be protected from all political affairs. But one of her maids reported that Mordecai was lying at the palace gates dressed in a robe of goat hair and covered by ashes. Esther was horrified. She sent the maid out to talk to Mordecai.

Mordecai gave a copy of Haman's order to the maid, asking her to tell Esther about the terror which had spread among

the Jews. He sent this message to Esther:
"Go to the king and tell him that you are
also Jewish. Plead with him to save the
lives of your people throughout his
empire."

Esther began to tremble from head to
foot when she received the message. She
sat down and scribbled a note to
Mordecai. "Everyone knows that the
queen cannot speak with the king unless
she has been asked. I could be put to
death just for seeking permission to see

18

him. I am afraid he is angry with me anyway."

But Mordecai begged in return, "Do you think that your life will be saved just because you are the queen? God can find someone else to help the Jews if you are afraid to speak up. But you and your family will be killed. Have faith, Esther! Perhaps God has made you queen for this very reason."

Esther sighed deeply and shuddered. The thought of coming before the king was scary enough, but to let him find out that his own wife was Jewish, and to ask him to reverse one of his own sealed commands was unthinkable. Her head drooped and tears began to pour from her eyes. No, she would never dare to do it.

Then, someone began to speak quietly to

Esther's heart. The voice became stronger and more urgent. At last, she could not ignore it, nor could she argue with the message: "Perhaps God has made you queen for this very reason."

Esther lifted her head and felt her spirits rise with it. "Return to Mordecai," she whispered to her maid. "Tell him to gather all the Jews in the city. Ask them to pray and go without food for three days. I will do the same. Then, even though it is forbidden, I will go to the king. If I am to die for my people, the Jews, then let it be so."

sther prayed continuously for three days just as she had promised. Then she rubbed sweet-smelling oils on her skin, put on her red gown and slowly made her way to the throne room where the king was sitting. She stopped just out of his sight and waited in the shadows. A dim lamp flickered against the wall. Her heart was pounding, but her dark eyes were steady and determined.

The king seemed to feel that she was there. The scent of her perfume filled the room. He turned his head slightly and saw her standing in the soft, shimmering light. She could never have imagined how lovely she looked. She was not aware of the grace with which she moved as she knelt before the king. Her beauty reawakened forgotten feelings in his heart.

The king lifted his golden scepter toward Esther. It was a sign that he welcomed her, a sign that she did not need to be afraid. Esther stepped closer and touched the tip of his scepter with her fingers. A look of tenderness passed between them.

"What is it, Esther? I will give you anything you wish, even the half of my kingdom," offered King Ahasuerus.

Esther's heart was pounding again. She did not feel peaceful in her spirit. She hesitated, lowered her eyes, and quietly answered, "I wish for the pleasure of your company at dinner this afternoon, together with Haman, your Chief of State."

"Yes, we would love to come. We will come as soon as we possibly can!" the king replied.

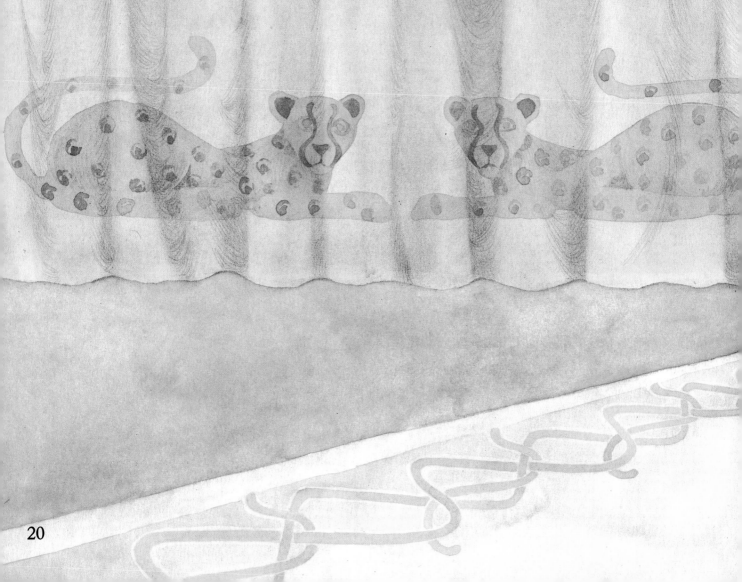

Later, when the three of them were sitting on their couches around the table, the king lifted his wine glass and said, "Come now, tell me, Esther. What is it you wish for me to give you? I will give you anything!"

The king's question once again made Esther feel uneasy. Something seemed to tell her that the time was not right to say what she had intended. Instead she answered, "I wish to enjoy the pleasure of your company here at my table again tomorrow. If you truly wish to make me happy, please come. Then I will tell you."

The two men left the table that day feeling satisfied and happy with themselves, especially Haman. At home he bragged to his family and servants that he had been to dinner with the king and queen, and had been invited again for the next day.

"But that miserable Mordecai!" Haman exclaimed. "Again today he refused to bow before me when I left the palace gates. It is humiliating!"

23

"He should be hanged immediately!"
Haman's wife declared.

"Good idea!" replied Haman. He ordered
a gallows built that very day and decided

to ask permission of the king first thing
the next morning.

However, that night the king woke up
and could not fall asleep again. Wanting
to put the time to good use, he began to
read his official record books. At dawn,

he was reading the part about the two officers of the Imperial Guard who had planned to kill him but whose plan was reported in time by a man named Mordecai.

"Has this Mordecai ever been rewarded?" he asked one of his aides at breakfast.

"No, but he still faithfully keeps watch at the palace gates."

Right then and there the king decided to do something to reward Mordecai. When Haman arrived for work that morning, King Ahasuerus met him at the door and asked, "Tell me, how should I reward a man who has won my favor?"

Haman thought to himself, "Who could have won the king's favor more than I?" So he answered, "Put your own royal robe on his shoulders and place a crown on his head. Let him sit upon your own horse as one of your most noble princes leads him through the streets shouting, 'This is the way the king rewards those who win his favor.' "

"A marvelous suggestion!" answered the king with a broad smile. "Here, you take this robe and crown, fetch my horse and go throughout the city leading Mordecai, the Jew upon it. Take care that you shout as loudly as you can, 'This is the way the king rewards those who win his favor!' "

Haman looked at the king in shock. It would never do to let the king know that he had intended to have Mordecai hanged to death that very day. Instead, Haman forced a faint smile upon his lips and nodded to the king. "Y-y-yes, Your Majesty," he stuttered. And so Haman was forced to do what the king had ordered.

That afternoon Haman showed up as expected at the queen's apartment for dinner. This time when the king asked Esther why she had invited them, Esther replied, "If you truly love me, then save my life and the lives of my people throughout the empire. For there is a decree that all Jews are to be killed on the 28th day of February this year."

"Who would order such a cruel thing?" demanded the king angrily.

"This man Haman," Esther replied softly.

The face of Haman turned ash-white, and he fell at Queen Esther's knees begging for mercy. King Ahasuerus was overcome by surprise. He stormed out of the room, then returned suddenly. Finding Haman still clinging to the queen, he became furious. He demanded that Haman be hanged that very day.

Esther began to weep. Tears spilled like raindrops down her pale cheeks. The worry and fear, the struggle for courage, and the decision for faith were all behind her now, but had made her weak. The king looked down and once again held out his golden scepter to Esther. At that moment she knew that, together, they would find a way to save the lives of the Jewish people.

29

Haman was hanged upon the very gallows
he had built for Mordecai. Mordecai
became Chief of State in Haman's place.
And from that day on, Esther grew in
favor with the king and as an influence
upon the affairs of the empire.

E sther found the courage to risk her
life by putting her faith in God. She
trusted his quiet voice and learned
that his timing is always perfect.